Irish Tourist Board

Bunratty Castle at Limerick, where medieval banquets are served.

THE SHANNON

River of Loughs and Legends

by NORA NOWLAN

Drawings by the Author
Maps by Fred Kliem

GARRARD PUBLISHING COMPANY
CHAMPAIGN, ILLINOIS

NANCY LARRICK, ED.D.,
IS THE EDUCATIONAL ADVISOR FOR THIS SERIES

For reading the manuscript of this book and checking
the accuracy of its content, the author and editor are
grateful to Mr. Thomas FitzGerald, M.A. Hons. Clas-
sics, H. Dip. in Ed., of Dublin, Ireland.

Manufactured in the United States of America
Library of Congress Catalog Number: 65-12285

Colonel Harry Rice

Morning mist veils an island in one of the Shannon's many loughs.

Contents

1. *Out of the Pot* 5

2. *The First People* 13

3. *The Singing Swans* 23

4. *Electricity from the Bogs* 30

5. *The Sergeant at the Bridge* 40

6. *The Lake with the Monster* 51

7. *The Lake of the Bloody Eye* 60

8. *Harnessing the River* 67

9. *Gateway to the Sea* 75

10. *West to the Atlantic* 86

Index 95

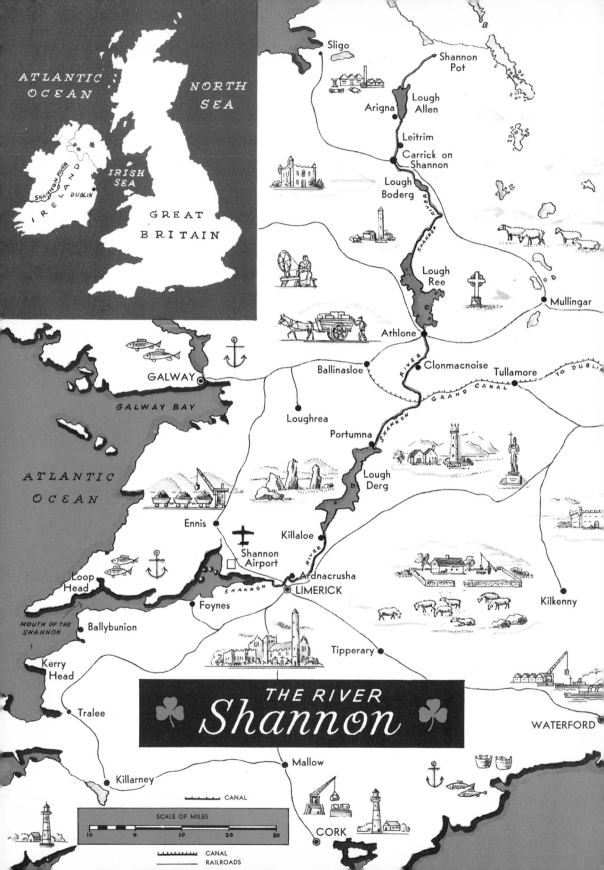

ATLANTIC
OCEAN

NORTH
SEA

SHANNON RIVER
IRELAND
DUBLIN

IRISH
SEA

GREAT
BRITAIN

Sligo

Shannon
Pot

Lough
Allen

Arigna

Leitrim

Carrick on
Shannon

Lough
Boderg

SHANNON RIVER

Lough
Ree

Mullingar

Athlone

GALWAY

Ballinasloe

Clonmacnoise

Tullamore

TO DUBLIN

GRAND CANAL

GALWAY BAY

Loughrea

Portumna

SHANNON

ATLANTIC
OCEAN

Lough
Derg

Ennis

Killaloe

RIVER

Shannon
Airport

Ardnacrusha
LIMERICK

Kilkenny

Loop
Head

SHANNON

Foynes

MOUTH OF THE
SHANNON

Ballybunion

Tipperary

Kerry
Head

THE RIVER
Shannon

Tralee

WATERFORD

Killarney

Mallow

CANAL

SCALE OF MILES

10   0   10   20   30

CORK

CANAL
RAILROADS

Gerald Kiely

The River Shannon begins in this pool, long known as the Shannon Pot.

1. **Out of the Pot**

The Shannon is a big river, the largest in Ireland and larger than any in Great Britain. It winds through the green heart of the country. Its story is also the story of Ireland and its people, their history and legends, their tears and their triumphs.

Ireland is a country of contrasts. Soft rains fall while the sun shines. Ancient round towers and smoking factory chimneys rise side by side against the skyline. Elegant long-legged foals graze next to shaggy donkeys, and thatched cottages hug the ground in the shadow of Norman castles.

Almost everyone in Ireland believes firmly in heaven and hell. There is also a lingering belief in a third kingdom inhabited by the Sidhe, the Little People. Legend says they were once rulers of the island but were conquered by the Gaels. They hid themselves deep down under the sea and under grassy mounds where they are said to live in beautiful palaces. Strange stories tell how the Little People help those they like and play evil tricks on any who meddle with places they claim as their own.

The Shannon takes its name from a fairy princess. She was Sineann, the lovely daughter of the king of the Land of Promise. This was a wonderful country where flowers never faded and nobody grew old. The princess went to seek the hazel bush of Wisdom and Poetry which grew by a well under the river. A wonderful bush it was, for the leaves and flowers and nuts all burst forth together and fell into the water, staining it a royal purple. Alas, the river was too strong for Sineann and she was drowned. But she left her name to the great river now called Shannon.

The river begins in the Shannon Pot, a pool about 50 feet across, in County Cavan. In summer the pool is clear and brown. Wild flowers and ferns cling to its mossy banks. In winter, when the rains are heavy and snows fall on the

Old-fashioned cottages with thatched roofs are scarce in Ireland now.

Irish Tourist Board

surrounding mountains, the pool seethes and bubbles like a witch's cauldron.

Underground streams flow down the mountains to feed the pool. The lonely countryside is a perfect hiding place for the makers of poteen, the bootleg whiskey of Ireland. Many a gallon of liquor has been distilled near the source of the Shannon. Time was when a telltale wisp of blue smoke could lead the police to a hidden still. After one successful raid, the policemen heaved a still and its contents into a small lake two miles above the Shannon Pot. The lake had no outlet on the surface. Not long afterward barley from the still was seen swirling around in the brown water of the Pot. Modern poteen makers are harder to catch. They use gas to boil their brew.

Ireland is something like a saucer. Its central limestone plain is surrounded by mountains. Through this central plain the Shannon makes its journey of about 220 miles to the Atlantic Ocean. From the Shannon Pot, 500 feet above sea level, the river falls rapidly until it reaches Lough Allen

8

A motorboat on the Shannon makes its way between rush-lined banks.

(lough is the Gaelic word for lake). Lough Allen, only a few miles from the Pot, is one of three large lakes fed by the Shannon. The others are Lough Ree and Lough Derg. Many other lakes are joined to the big river by tributaries. They form a silver web connecting the Shannon's sprawling waters.

For 190 miles below Lough Allen, the river falls an average of only four inches a mile and often

The hart's-tongue fern is rare in the U.S.A.

seems scarcely to move at all. When the moon
is full, its reflection in the water is quite still,
like a great golden dish. The only way to find
out which way the river is flowing is by throwing
a reed or stick into the water.

Twelve miles above Limerick the river begins
to tumble down. It spins the turbines of the
hydroelectric plant at Ardnacrusha and flows
through Limerick. Then it broadens into a wide

estuary, which runs 60 miles to the Atlantic Ocean.

The Shannon is a clean river. Few factories and only two important towns, Athlone and Limerick, are on its banks. Because there is no pollution, water plants flourish. This abundance of plant life provides food and oxygen for the vast population of fish and tiny creatures of the water. The lakes of the Shannon have hundreds of islands, most of them inhabited by birds that can nest undisturbed by cats and other prowlers.

In summer the golden gorse blazes on the banks, and in autumn the purple heather glows on the brown bogland. Swans glide majestically on the calm water, and larks soar and sing in the soft air. Tall reeds stand motionless like sentinels at the water's edge, and willows brush the river with gray-green leaves. On stormy winter nights the curlew's lonely cry is blown across the desolate river.

Before man made roads, the Shannon was the highway of Ireland. Because it is deep and slow and flows through the central plain, all kinds of people have used it. The boats of the earliest travelers were hollowed from tree trunks. One of these ancient boats is in the National Museum in Dublin. It is 52 feet long and was made from an oak tree. Other boats had frames of willow, ash or birch saplings, covered with hides. The boats had no keels and could be used in shallow water.

More than a thousand years ago the Shannon brought unwelcome visitors to Ireland. These were the Vikings from Norway and Denmark, who sailed to foreign harbors to trade or plunder. They were also known as Norsemen and Danes. The Vikings swept up the river in their long, black boats, murdered the inhabitants, burned their houses and carried away everything of value. For many years the word Viking sounded like a death knell to those who dwelt by the Shannon.

Today the people live as peacefully as the river flows. There is always time to dream and dawdle, to tell a tale or listen to one. Anyone who seems in too great a hurry is told gently, "Take your time, now. Didn't the Man Above who made time make plenty of it?"

2. The First People

When the Shannon leaves the Pot, it is only a little river, just wide enough for a brown-legged boy or a small black calf to jump over.

County Cavan, where the river begins, is a county of little hills and little lakes and small black cattle. The farms are poor and cannot feed large cattle, so the calves are sold as yearlings. The soil is black and acid, and the land is swampy and hilly. Oats and potatoes are grown in small fields tilled with a horse or donkey plow, or dug with a spade. Hay is cut and saved for winter fodder. Tucked away from the wind and the weather are whitewashed farm houses, mostly thatched with oaten straw. Like gold they shine when the sun touches them.

About two miles from the Pot the Shannon is joined by a larger stream, the Owenmore River. Grown quite suddenly into a big river, the

A cauldron of bronze sheets riveted together, made about 700 B.C.

Shannon spills into Lough Allen, which is six miles long and surrounded by bleak mountains. Streams pour into the lake from all sides. On the vivid green slopes they gleam like silver-satiny ribbons.

When the river was harnessed at Ardnacrusha for electric power, the lake was used as a reservoir. The outlet was deepened. In dry weather the sluice gates were opened to provide water for the power station far below. Miles of golden sands appeared where the water had been. On the sands and at the lake edge were found relics of far-off days. From these relics and from other studies, archaeologists made a picture of how the first people lived. Stone axes, flint knives and choppers told of trees that were cut. Bone fishhooks, fish

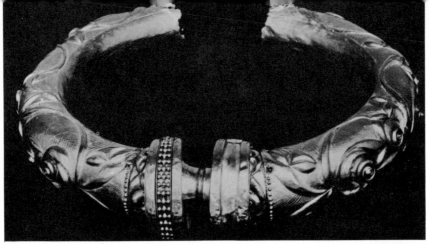

Goldsmiths of the 1st century A.D. fashioned this hollow necklet.

spears and net-sinkers told of fish in the river.

The ancient Irish were a pastoral people who lived chiefly by their herds of cattle and swine, which found rich pasture on the riverbanks. The country was then covered with huge forests. The National Museum has the complete skeleton of a giant deer or elk twice as tall as a man and with a horn span of 11 feet. These animals lived in the Ice Age and were extinct before the first people hunted wolves, wild boars and red deer in the forests.

Some people lived in crannogs, the ancient lake dwellings. A crannog was an artificial island made by sinking a platform of woven branches or brushwood in shallow water. The platform was weighted with stones, and a round house was built on it. The house had a wooden frame plastered with clay and a thatched roof made with rushes. Generally the family used a boat to reach the shore, but sometimes a causeway was built with stones which ran zigzag just below the water. A stranger approaching at night would miss his footing and tumble into the lake. The men felt their women and children were safe in the crannogs while they hunted, fished and cared for their beasts.

The women kept house in their own fashion. Household articles were made of stone, horn, clay, bronze and copper. Clay pots were often decorated with designs made with shells, twisted cords and birds' feet.

The discovery of coal made life easier for the first people. It was dug from Arigna Mountain and used to smelt copper ore. But copper was too soft to make good knives and tools. Later the secret of mixing tin with copper to make bronze was learned. Bronze was hard, and served well for tools and weapons, ornaments and pots. Gold was found in the rivers and hammered into beautiful ornaments. These prehistoric people had great skill as designers and metalworkers.

In about 350 B.C. the Celts or Gaels came to Ireland from Central Europe through Spain. There is a legend that travelers had told them of the green fertile island and its store of gold. The Celts were expert ironworkers, and their iron weapons made it easy for them to conquer the country. Storytellers say it was then that the Little People were driven underground, where they have lived ever since.

The Celts mined iron ore from the Iron Mountain close to the Shannon Pot. They cut down trees, built roads, reared animals and tilled the soil with iron plows. On the banks of the river they built forts. A group of several houses was surrounded by a stone wall or earthen bank with a gate or bridge. These forts, called raths or duns, gave protection against enemies and wild beasts. The ruins of many can still be seen, and their names have been kept in place names. Rathmore means "the big rath" and Dunmore means "the big dun."

Shaggy Irish wolfhounds, with a lady who wears a shaggy Irish sweater.

The men hunted with wolfhounds, famous for their strength, intelligence and courage. These rough-coated dogs, white or brindle, stand 30 inches high. Olaf, a Norwegian, was the son of an Irish princess. He says to his friend Ogumnar in an ancient saga:

"I will give thee a hound was given me in

Ireland. He is big and no worse than a stout man. Besides it is part of his nature that he has a man's wit, and he will bay at every man whom he knows to be thy foe, but never at thy friends. He can see too in a man's face if he means thee well or ill and he will lay down his life to be true to thee. The dog's name is Sam."

Wolfhounds are still bred in Ireland. Many are shipped to America and to Africa where they are used as guard dogs.

St. Patrick, Ireland's patron saint, was brought to the country as a captive by a band of Irish raiders who had ventured into England. He was then only about 16. After six years of bondage he escaped in a ship carrying wolfhounds to Europe. Many years later he returned to Ireland as a bishop to preach Christ's gospel. On one of his journeys he crossed the Shannon at Drumsna near Lough Allen. The tradition is that St. Patrick drove all of the demons and snakes out of Ireland. Certain it is that there are no snakes in the country, but we cannot be sure about demons.

On the lonely western shore of the lake a plume of white vapor streams across the sky. It comes from the Arigna Generating Station which burns pulverized coal from the same mountains that fired the furnaces of the ancient metalworkers.

Lough Allen is full of fish. Each year competitions are held to catch the biggest pike and perch. These fish eat quantities of salmon and trout, and the aim is to get rid of as many as possible. Brown trout also eat a lot of salmon fry. The young salmon are marked with tags at the hatchery, and 28 tags were found in the stomach of one trout. Because Irish folk like to catch and eat brown trout, the fish are forgiven for the damage they do to salmon.

The competitions are great sport, attracting fishermen from England, France and other countries. Everyone can join in. A foreign angler with expensive gear will find himself beside a barefoot boy with a homemade rod, and sometimes the delighted schoolboy hauls in the biggest fish.

Pike are not often eaten in Ireland, but in France they are a delicacy. A pike may weigh

St. Patrick hurls his bell at the demons, as seen by an ancient artist.

National Library

Mitellus f.

25 or 30 pounds. It is bronze green, with a long snout and cruel jaws. Some fishermen say pike move too slowly to catch healthy fish and do good by killing weak or sickly trout.

Perch travel in shoals and eat anything they can swallow. They lay their eggs in sticky strings near the riverbank Some stick to the legs of wading birds and are carried out into the river or to other streams. Fishermen often find strings of eggs attached to submerged branches. They remove them, to help keep down the perch population.

Children fish for pinkeens, the Gaelic name for minnows. The little fish are kept in jars or preserved in salt for use as bait. Another bait is the grub of the bluebottle fly. The flies are put in a box until they lay their eggs. When the grubs hatch, they are fed on meat until they are big enough to interest a fish. The youngsters call these grubs "channelers." Many a fat trout has been caught with one—out of season or in preserved water by a young poacher.

3. The Singing Swans

Swans are everywhere on the Shannon. They are mute swans, pure white with graceful necks. When they are disturbed, the male, or "cob," makes a kind of grunt and a distinctive papery noise with his wings. The female hisses softly.

They do not mate until they are three years old, and they stay together for life. The cob and the "pen," or female, seek out a site on a lake or canal, stake their claim and build their nest. Once they have settled, woe betide any other male who foolishly tries to jump their claim. The intruder will be held with his head under water until he is half drowned and so scared that he makes off as soon as he is released.

The nest built, the pair raises a family of four to six cygnets each year. The young birds are gray and far from beautiful until they are almost a year old. While the mother ferries the little lazy ones on her back, the father sails around like an escorting destroyer. Very grand he looks with his neck arched and his wings curving stiffly away from his body. He will attack anyone who interferes with his nest or his family and will even kill a dog bigger than himself.

In the Shannon estuary there are hundreds of swans. These are the teen-agers, the spinsters and bachelors, and the old birds who have lost their mates. The cygnets stay with their parents until the next nesting season; then they are driven away and join up with the flocks on the estuary. To see a great gathering of these beautiful birds on the seashore is a wonderful sight.

Swans live on water plants and do not kill fish. Nobody ever interferes with them, and they increase in number every year. Indeed it is thought unlucky to kill a swan.

One May morning when the hedges were white and sweet with hawthorn and the blackbirds were singing, three men went fishing for salmon on the banks of Lough Boderg. Down a smooth sheet of water flew three swans like three gleaming white

24

Three cygnets and their mother in a nest by the Shannon.
Irish Tourist Board

seaplanes landing in formation. One of the men was holding a gun.

"They scare the fish," called one of the others. "Seamus, fire a shot!" The gun was raised. The shot was fired hastily but, alas, too accurately. There was a tumult of beating wings as the center bird struggled for its life. Weaker and weaker it became, then sank slowly under the brown water. The two remaining swans made off downstream. There was silence, and nothing to be seen but a drift of white feathers on the water. No one spoke. The face of Seamus was full of misery. One of the others found his tongue. "Forget it," he said gruffly. " 'Twas a mistake." He picked up his rod. A puff of cloud covered the sun and a chill little wind ruffled the calm water. The men shivered. Maybe each was thinking of the story of the children of Lir.

All good stories begin "Once upon a time," so: Once upon a time there was a chieftain called Lir. His wife was very beautiful, and he loved her very much. They had four children, three sons and a daughter called Fionnuala. Lir's lovely wife died, and he was left with the four children to bring up. He was so fond of them that he worried lest he fail to look after them properly. Then he did a foolish thing.

He went to a king who was a wizard and lived on a lake in the Shannon. His name was Bov Dearg, and he had a daughter named Eva. Lir arranged with the king that Eva would marry him and mind the children for him.

Lir made such a fuss over his children that Eva became mad with jealousy. She thought up a way to get rid of them. One day she took them riding in her chariot and ordered her servants to kill them. The servants refused. Then Eva told them to drive on to a lake. She had learned witchcraft from her father, and when the children went in to bathe she turned them into four snow-white swans.

Fionnuala spoke up and said, "You will be punished for this wickedness without a doubt, but tell me how long must we remain swans?" "Nine hundred years," said Eva. But she was sorry for this thing she had done, and she said unhappily,

"I cannot now undo this evil, but you will be able to think and to speak as before, and you will be able to sing the most beautiful songs ever heard. The day you hear a church bell ringing you will be released from the spell."

When the story became known, the king made a law forbidding anyone to harm a swan. Fionnuala and her brothers went from place to place for nine hundred years. They sang wonderful songs which were sad and wild yet strangely sweet. The notes were as soft and pure as the down on their own lovely necks. All who heard them were bewitched. The children's eyes sparkled and laughter bubbled from their lips. The grownups forgot their troubles and were filled with a great peace, the like of which they had never known before.

One day Fionnuala and her brothers heard a bell tolling across the water. They hastened to the shore and found a little church. They went up onto the shore. The feathers fell from them, and there stood three ancient old men and an ancient old woman. The priest of the church listened to their story and cared for them. Later he told them the story of Christ and baptized them. Not long afterward they died.

As for Eva, Lir was so angry with her that he forbade her to come near him again. Worse was to come. Her father, Bov Dearg, was so furious that he turned her into a horrible demon and condemned her to wander through the sky forever.

It is said that like a great raggedy crow she sometimes flies over her father's lake, darkening the setting sun for an instant with her shadow and letting out long screams of rage and misery. Others say it is only a gray heron or a curlew that flies calling and crying across the purple sky. Who can tell?

Since Eva's day, Ireland has replaced chariots with Diesel trains.

Irish Tourist Board

Irish Turf Board

Lanesborough Bridge across the Shannon. This bridge was built for trains hauling turf from the bog (dark area) to the power station.

4. Electricity from the Bogs

About one-sixth of Ireland is covered with peat bogs. The Shannon flows through part of this vast swampy area.

Bogs are formed by the growth and decay of water plants. The most important of these is sphagnum, or bog moss. Wherever water lies, crops of moss grow up quickly and decay as quickly. They are replaced by more moss. Over many years the decayed moss becomes tightly packed by the weight of water and the layers of moss above. It turns into peat, or turf. The brown turf is almost as solid as wood and is burned for heat and cooking.

Turf has been forming for thousands and thousands of years. In some places the bog is 40 feet deep, but generally the depth is much less. Most bogs are springy and pleasant to walk on, but some, called quaking bogs, are feared and avoided by all. These swamps are found in the middle of ordinary bogs. Anyone who treads on them will sink and disappear if help is not near. Many a man has gone out at night to seek a stray animal and has never been heard of again. Quaking bogs hold many secrets and do not give up their victims.

Turf cutters make strange discoveries. The acid peat has preservative qualities. Human skeletons dressed in leather and woolen clothes of hundreds

A farmer cutting turf. He is using a spade-like tool called a slane.

of years ago have been found. Another interesting find was "bog butter." It seems to have been the custom to bury butter in summer when it was plentiful and dig it up for use in winter. The butter was put in leather, wooden or wicker containers and sunk in the cool bogs. Sometimes

The Turf Board's machine lifts the sods and piles them for drying.

the butter got lost, like a nut buried by a squirrel. After a couple of hundred years it would still be recognizable as unsalted butter.

Turf has long been harvested, or "won," by hand along the banks of the Shannon. Many farms have turbary rights. This is the right to

33

Bringing home the dried sods by donkey-power. Note the boy's switch.

cut a given amount of turf from an adjoining bog each year.

In May the turf is cut into brick-size blocks, or sods, with a spade-like tool called a slane. Like chunks of mud, the turf is laid out to dry. Later the sods are piled into heaps for further drying. When most of the water has gone, the turf is

This Turf Board machine loads a long pile of sods into railway cars.

carted home by horse or donkey cart. If the turf
bank is far from a road and the bog too soft for
cart wheels, donkeys haul the sods in wicker
baskets hung from pegs on a wooden straddle.
Sometimes a braided straw mat is thrown over the
donkey's back to keep the baskets from hurting
its sides.

35

Once home, the turf is stacked into ricks near the house and thatched with straw or field rushes to keep out rain. Some of the ricks are bigger than the houses.

Turf is burned on a flat open hearth. This used to be the only means of cooking or of warming the house. Almost every house now has an electric cooker or a turf-burning cooker, but it is around the blazing hearth that the family gathers. In some farmhouses it is the proud boast that the fire has never gone out in more than a hundred years. Each night a few sods are completely covered with ashes. Next morning the ash is gently raked away and the seed of the fire blown to life with a bellows.

Nowadays turf production is a thriving industry. During World War II fuel was very scarce, for little coal is mined in Ireland. Many bogs which had lain idle for years were opened up to supply much of the country's fuel. The government set up a Turf Board to develop the peat resources of the country. The board bought 100,000 acres of bog and began to harvest turf by machinery.

Machine-winning of turf is basically the same as the old-fashioned method—but the machines work on acres producing thousands of tons instead of on banks producing donkey loads. The turf is scooped out of the bog by a machine using a great bucket. It goes through another machine which grinds it up and compresses it into long strips. The strips are passed on to the drying ground. Discs then cut each strip into about 140 sods. When they dry enough, they are ready to burn.

Electricity is now generated with turf as a fuel. At Lanesborough, on the north end of Lough Ree, is the country's first turf-fired generating station. Steam is made in boilers heated with turf fires. The steam is used to turn the dynamos that make electricity.

Milled peat is also used in power stations. The peat is milled or minced up on the bog by machine. Next it is harrowed to hasten drying. The dry crumbly peat is then ready to heat the boilers. Milled peat is also compressed into briquettes for use in houses. So up-to-date are the

Turf Board's methods that technicians have come from the Soviet Union and Pakistan to study them.

No picture of Shannon's boglands would be complete without mention of the donkeys seen along the banks, in the fields and on the roads. Donkeys, white, black, brown and gray are everywhere. Early in the nineteenth century, England needed many, many horses for her armies in Europe. The generals looked westward. In Ireland were plenty of the best horses in the world. So the generals bought Spanish donkeys and forced the Irish farmers to exchange their horses at the rate of two donkeys for every horse. The Irish did not like this but had no choice. As it turned out, it was not such a bad bargain.

Donkeys are ideal for small farms. They can do almost as much work as a horse on far less food. They can pull a heavy load and can be handled by quite small children. They pull a flat cart to the creamery with milk, they haul fodder and turf, they are ridden to school by children. Even Grandpa will ride the ass to the village store for his tobacco and a bit of a chat. Although they often look ill-used and unfortunate, like cats they are well able to look after themselves.

Almost every country child has discovered how hard it is to stay on a barebacked donkey who has decided he is tired of his rider. It is head down, heels up and away goes the donkey alone. When a donkey decides to stop, he stops. That donkey and nobody else decides what is going to happen next.

5. The Sergeant at the Bridge

There are two large towns on the Shannon: Athlone and Limerick. Athlone is at the southern end of Lough Ree. It is the gateway to Connacht, the stronghold of the native Irish during the 600 years of English domination of the country.

Henry II, the English king, was also king of Normandy in France. Henry's followers, the Normans, began coming to Ireland in 1169. The Normans were Catholics, and in time they married into Irish families and became "more Irish than the Irish." When Henry VIII of England broke with the Church of Rome, he and his successors persecuted the Irish Catholics. They made laws penalizing those who would not become Protestants.

The rich lands of the Catholics were given to English planters by Queen Elizabeth and by Oliver Cromwell in the seventeenth century. When

Cromwell was asked, "But where will the Irish go?" he answered sharply: "They can go to hell or to Connacht."

Connacht's barren acres thus became their stronghold. Here the impoverished but proud Irish starved, plotted, prayed, schemed and fought to regain the lands of their fathers. There was much blood spilt, many tears shed and hearts broken before the dream of Ireland ruled by Irishmen was to come true in 1922.

Athlone is built on both sides of the river and has only one road bridge. Although it is a busy town, it is a country town. Factories there are, and thriving woolen mills, but the impatient motorist must bide his time as the cows wander through the streets at milking time.

Donkey carts are parked beside fast automobiles. People stroll and chat on the sidewalks. The motorist hooting at a cart gets a cheery wave from the driver and an amused look which seems to say, "God give ye sense, let ye take yer time," as he hauls on the rope reins and pulls to the side.

There is a proverb which says, "When you cross the Shannon at Athlone, throw away your watch and use a calendar."

Over the roofs hangs a blue haze of turf smoke, and its acrid smell fills the air.

Much of the business of the town is done by boat. A man casually rows downstream with a wriggling sack on board. A calf's head pokes out of the sack and a mournful "Moo!" comes over the water. A bearded, cowled friar scuds by in an outboard motor boat. Bales of wool, cargoes of grain, turf or potatoes are loaded and unloaded as they have been for hundreds of years.

Floating hotels, made from old barges, are berthed at Athlone. They take guests for cruises on the lakes. Cabin cruisers carry holiday makers and fishermen to their destinations.

Athlone has always been of great military importance in Irish history. The Siege of Athlone and the Battle at the Bridge are remembered with pride by the Irish.

In 1690 the town was besieged by the forces of William III of England. The garrison was

The railway bridge on the Shannon at Athlone, gateway to Connacht.

This steam train was on a branch line to Loughrea, west of Athlone.

commanded by Colonel Richard Grace who, when asked his terms of surrender, fired a pistol in the air and said, "These are my terms. These only shall I give or receive. When my provisions are consumed, I shall defend my trust until I have eaten my boots."

The following year, Athlone was again besieged by the English. The Irish retired after blowing up two arches of the bridge. The English tried to make repairs but the Irish, led by the gallant Sergeant Custume, went out eight at a time and tore the planks away with their bare hands, losing many men. Seeing that their task was impossible, the English tried another ruse. They sent three foreign mercenaries—already under death sentence—into the river to find a shallow fording place, then fired over their heads. The Irish thought that three Irishmen had escaped and held their fire. The prisoners gained the Connacht bank and the English poured after them, routing the gallant defenders. The stone barracks overlooking the bridge are called Custume barracks, in memory of the sergeant.

44

In 1697 Athlone castle, used as a magazine, was struck by lightning. Three hundred barrels of gunpowder blew up, burning most of the town.

Nine miles south of Athlone, on a desolate and sluggish stretch of the river, is Clonmacnoise. It was once one of the most famous monastic cities in Europe. The only remains today are the ruins of seven churches, two round towers and great stone crosses. It was here that St. Ciaran founded his monastery in 548 A.D. To it came wise and holy men from war-scarred Europe, hoping to find peace of mind and body.

Here were written books which became famous for their beauty and craftsmanship, treasured today by the few libraries which have them. For five hundred years, sanctity, art and learning flourished in Clonmacnoise. Many missionaries sailed down the Shannon on their way to preach the gospel in far lands.

A city grew up around the monastery. In it the most skilled craftsmen built stone churches and decorated them with cut stone and lovely carved designs.

Books were written by hand with goose-quill pens. They were written on vellum with inks made from the galls, known as "oak apples," which grow on oak trees. Vellum is calfskin, stretched on a frame, scraped and limed. Parchment is made in the same way but from sheepskin. The books were gorgeously decorated with inks colored red with red lead, green with verdigris, yellow with sulphur and blue with lapis lazuli. Lapis lazuli came from Asia and was most precious. It took two or three years of a man's life to bring a supply of it to Ireland. The scribes ornamented their manuscripts, written in the Latin or Gaelic language, with huge capital letters. Some of the interlaced work is so fine that it could only have been drawn with a single hair.

Into the designs they drew strange and often comical birds, beasts and fishes. Some of those portrayed are familiar today. From their expressions it seems that the artists smiled and their eyes twinkled as they drew.

Books were very precious. They were held as ransom and exchanged for tracts of land and

A Celtic cross and a round tower
stand in the ruins of Clonmacnoise.
Irish Board of Works

herds of cattle. Yet the writers often scribbled little notes on the margins, telling of their joys and fears. That they became sad and impatient, hungry and frightened, is told in these notes.

One scribe cursed roundly the cleaning women "who have mixed up my inks, my colouring matters and books. The curse of God on them and on all those who read this without cursing them." Another wrote that he was glad that it was stormy and the waves high, as there was no fear of a raid by the Danes. Another poor fellow complained, "It's tired I am today and the screaming of the children in the house outside annoying me."

From the sixth to the ninth centuries was the golden age of art and culture by the Shannon. Ireland became known as the Island of Saints and Scholars.

In the ninth century the Vikings made their way up the river. St. Ciaran's monastery, standing by the slow-moving river, was frequently plundered. The monks built round watchtowers and used them as belfries and places of refuge.

Culver Pictures Inc.
Viking raiders came to Ireland in ships like this.

Round towers like these are not found anywhere else in the world. They were built of stone and are 40 to 60 feet around the base, 60 to 120 feet high, tapering slightly and with a conical stone roof. The door was 10 to 15 feet above ground level. Each tower was divided into four floors with a window at each floor and four at the top.

When the black-sailed Viking ships were sighted, the people hurried to the towers with their treasures. They climbed the ladder, pulled it up after them and barred the door. Then they waited until the dreaded marauders had sailed away, leaving smouldering ruins behind. The monks provided themselves with large stones which they dropped onto any enemies who came within range.

This state of affairs lasted for over a hundred years. When the Danes were defeated, the Normans came. The country was unsettled and unhappy. The people were continually under arms, with little time for building, art or learning.

St. Matthew, as painted by ancient Irish monks in the Book of Kells.

Fred Kliem

6. The Lake with the Monster

Below Lanesborough the Shannon enters Lough Ree, which is 16 miles long. Geologists think it was once an underground lake and that centuries ago the limestone roof collapsed, leaving huge caverns more than 100 feet deep.

It is a mysterious lake, and no one has ever explored its depths. In the life of St. Mochua, one of the early saints, there is an account of "a stag who took refuge on an island in Lough Ree. None dared to follow him on account of a horrible monster with a mane and tail which infested the lake and was accustomed to destroy swimmers. At last a man went across but as he returned the beast devoured him."

St. Ciaran, who lived on the Shannon at Clonmacnoise, fell out with the monster because the beast didn't like bells ringing and monks singing. The saint won the battle and is supposed to have tied up the monster and put him in the bottom of the lake, where he must stay until the end of the world.

But is there a monster? And if there is, has he stayed on the bottom? Consider the strange thing that happened to three priests who were fishing on a fine evening in May, 1960. They were sitting in a boat, waiting for the trout to rise. About 80 yards away a large, snake-like creature broke water and moved slowly along the still lake, taking no heed of the men in the boat. It stayed above water for two or three minutes, submerged quietly and then rose again. This time it was visible long enough for one of the watchers to sketch it. Again it disappeared and was not seen again.

The sketch and a report of what happened were sent to learned men who have studied rare monsters for years. The scientists replied that strange creatures might indeed live in the caverns of a deep lake like Lough Ree. There is rich vegetation in the bottom of the lake and plenty of food for fish and other creatures. One expert,

The Shannon monster is bashful, unlike this Canadian terror of 1872.

Lionel Leslie, a Fellow of the Royal Geographical Society, had this to say: "As an authority on the Loch Ness (Scotland) monster, I am interested in a recent confidential report by reliable witnesses concerning an animal of no known species having been seen in a large lough in southern Ireland. . . . I see no reason why a smaller relative should not exist in at least one of the larger sized loughs in Ireland because no one has ever seen the bottom of it and therefore cannot have any idea what forms of life inhabit its deeper waters."

Everyone seems to agree that these creatures

53

are timid and do not have manes. They are not likely to make a meal out of people who swim in Lough Ree.

During the ninth century Ireland was plagued by the Vikings. One of the most terrible raiders was Turgesius the Dane. He and his robbers sailed up the Shannon and captured a fort on Lough Ree called Rindoon. For 13 years Turgesius ruled there, terrorizing the natives and growing rich on plunder. He was without mercy, and he was full of vanity.

There was at that time an Irish king in Meath called Malachy. He had a beautiful daughter. Turgesius fell in love with her and commanded Malachy to send her to his fort at Lough Ree. Malachy knew it would be dangerous to refuse, but he and his daughter thought up a plan. The king sent a messenger saying his daughter would visit Turgesius, and she would travel as befitted a princess, with 14 serving women. Then the king chose 14 of his strongest, fairest and youngest warriors and dressed them as women. The party arrived at nightfall. The Danes had a feast for the handsome women and put aside their swords.

Suddenly the maidens threw off their flowing garments, pulled forth their weapons and set upon the unarmed Danes. Malachy, who was secretly waiting outside with more warriors, rushed the gates. He killed or captured the rest of Turgesius's band. Turgesius himself was taken prisoner, and Malachy ordered him to be bound in chains and thrown into a lake. The power of the Danes was broken for a time, and it is said that every Irishman living on Lough Ree had a Danish slave to do his bidding.

People travel by boat on Lough Ree as casually as a schoolboy by bicycle. They explore the coves and bays and the wooded islands. Fifty of the islands are named, and many have the ruins of ancient churches and other buildings. Holy people used to go to these peaceful places to pray and to study. They ate birds, fish and rabbits. Cattle gave them milk, meat and leather. Sheep were also eaten, their milk made into cheese and their wool spun and woven into cloth. Trees provided fuel and wood for building.

A group of islands called the Black Islands is still inhabited. Their people live by fishing for eels and by grazing cattle. The cattle swim from island to island as they please. They are brought home and to market by tying a rope around their horns and guiding them behind a flat-bottomed boat called a "cot."

The country is so flat that it floods badly in winter and animals must be moved to higher ground. The fields below flood level are called "callows." Animals graze in them right down to

A basket made with rushes cut from Lough Ree.

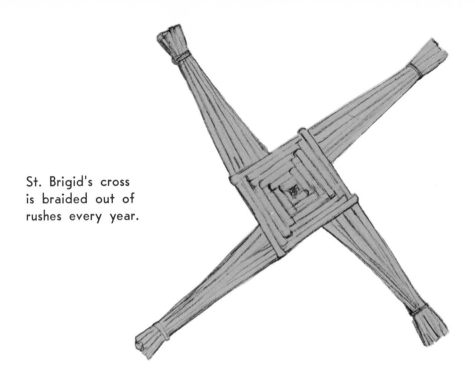

St. Brigid's cross is braided out of rushes every year.

the edge of the water. Along the banks are disappearing ponds known as "turloughs." After heavy rain a pond will vanish as though by magic. The bottom of a turlough has cracks which fill up with dead leaves and weeds. A heavy rain washes out the vegetation, and the water runs away as though a plug had been pulled out. The turloughs empty into underground streams which flow into the river.

Rushes are gathered from the river for making into baskets and mats. In summer, men and boys wade out into the rush beds, cut the rushes and

Irish Tourist Board

The friendly Shannon provides the background for a musical afternoon.

float them back to the bank on rafts. Women and children gather them into bundles and put them to dry. Then they are woven into baskets around slim willow branches.

It is an ancient custom among country folk to

hang a rush cross in the house on February 1 in honor of St. Brigid, the patroness of Ireland. The belief is that she will take the farm under her care and bring peace and plenty to the family. Brigid was a king's daughter. When her golden cross was stolen, she braided one of rushes. "For," said she, "no one will bother to steal this one." The St. Brigid's cross is so well known in Ireland that it is used as the symbol of Telefís Eireann, the nation's television service.

Nowadays the waters of Lough Ree resound to the hum of motorboats. Water skiers flash past, and great houseboats which were once canal barges throb their way among the islands. Fishermen cast their lines and haul at their nets. Bird watchers patiently wait for a glimpse of the rare birds which nest on the quiet islands, and botanists scour them in search of unusual plants. Swimmers dive into the brown water, and everywhere the friendly Shannon welcomes all who come.

7. The Lake of the Bloody Eye

Flat, broad and slow, the river meanders on, and at Shannon Harbour is joined by the Grand Canal. The canal is hardly used at all now, but before there were railroads it was very important because it connected the Shannon with Dublin, the capital city. One could travel right across the country by water.

First-class passenger travel was done in narrow metal boats known as fly boats because of their speed. They made about eight miles per hour, drawn by four horses galloping along the towpath. If the horses were changed often, the boat could reach Shannon Harbour in a day. The passengers stayed there overnight and went on next day by boat or in a long car, a kind of stagecoach. Cargo and turf went in barges drawn by one horse plodding along the towpath. The gaunt gray shell of the once busy hotel still stands at

A stone wall bars a donkey (arrow) from a hayfield on Lough Derg.

the harbor. Houseboats and pleasure craft are moored there in winter.

At Portumna the river enters Lough Derg. Thousands of years ago learned storytellers called bards used to travel the land, telling the news and entertaining the people with stories and songs. These men were very powerful. If they did not think they had been properly treated, they could ruin their host's good name. One of these bards, named Ahirny, was feared and hated because of his spiteful tongue, and the chieftains took great trouble to please him. It happened that he came to the great fort of a king near this lake. The king had only one eye. Ahirny was given the best of everything. To be sure that his hospitality was well spoken of, the king told the bard to name anything that he wished and it would be given him. Maliciously, Ahirny demanded his host's remaining eye. There was little the poor man could do but gouge it out and hand it over.

His servants led him to the lake to bathe the gaping socket. As he stood up, one of his servants noticed that the whole surface of the lake was blood red. He told his master. Standing there on the crimson shore, the king declared, "From this day let the lake be known as Lough Dergderc—the Lake of the Bloody Eye."

Lough Derg, as it is now called, is about 22 miles long. The Danes built a fleet there, and it has carried Norman and English invaders over its shining waters. Each spring and summer there comes a happier invasion when many families come to this holiday lake. Some rent houseboats or cabin cruisers; others live in floating hotels which cruise along the river. Caravans, or trailers, can park almost anywhere if the driver just asks the landowner's permission.

One of the favorite places for picnics is at Killaloe, which has the remains of an ancient palace called Kincora. It was the summer home of Brian Boru, who in 1014 rid Ireland of the threat of Danish conquest.

One of the really exciting times at Lough Derg comes in the "dapping" season of spring. Dapping is fishing for trout with the mayfly. Like the beat of tom-toms in a jungle, the message "the fly is up on Derg" is heard as far away as Dublin and London. Anglers hastily make arrangements for a fishing holiday. Rod and gear are hauled out, lines tangle in vacuum cleaners, children sit on fishhooks and everyone is nearly driven mad before the fishermen set off.

Independent Newspapers Ltd.

The little town of Killaloe is a favorite spot for Lough Derg picnics.

The mayfly hatches earlier on Lough Derg than on the other Shannon lakes, but nobody ever knows quite when the hatch will be. The grubs lie all winter in the bottom of the lake. Suddenly thousands of them float to the surface where they stay for a short time. The protecting case splits and the fly crawls out. It flies downwind to the banks where it hides in the bushes.

All day long the flies stay quite still. At dusk they rise like myriads of glittering sequins in their

64

mating dance. Then the males fall to the ground. The females flutter out onto the water, where they lay their eggs and die. The fisherman goes along the bank picking up the flies and putting them in a ventilated box. This is his bait.

Dapping is done from a boat which drifts downwind. The fine line baited with a shining fly blows and dances on the surface. The trout go mad. They dash into the shallows grabbing at each insect. Anyone can go dapping and stand a good chance of catching trout—even with only a bent pin and willow sapling. After three weeks the trout will not look at a mayfly but go chasing after shoals of perch fry.

On summer evenings there is plenty of time to talk over the day's doings, the fishing and the sailing. Everyone in Ireland loves to hear or to tell a story. There are singsongs in the house or in the local public house where the holiday makers go to buy supplies. In Ireland the village store sells everything from liquor to shoelaces, from bacon to postage stamps, and it has a wonderful smell all its own.

It is the children's job to fetch milk and eggs from nearby farms. They set off in the evening, often barefooted, through the dewy grass to the whitewashed houses where the hens, ducks and geese poke around the half door. Satiny mushrooms grow in the fields and are there for the taking. They are carried home threaded on long stiff pieces of dry grass. They are good cooked on top of the stove with salt.

At dusk little white moths flicker over the lake. Spiders spin gossamer webs between the reeds, and the dew hangs diamonds on them. There is a smell of wood smoke. A boat grinds on the stones. Cheerful voices bid each other goodnight and feet swish through the grass. A fish plops. A moorhen scutters across the water. A dog barks, and one by one the lights go out on the banks and on the water.

Another day and a good one has been added to the long story of the Lake of the Bloody Eye.

8. Harnessing the River

At the southern end of Lough Derg the Shannon narrows again, and at Killaloe the river builds up to turn the turbines at Ardnacrusha power station.

A government report of 1844 said the 100 feet of fall between Killaloe and Limerick could produce 33,950 horsepower throughout the year. Electricity was unheard of in those days. The weight and power of water turned mill wheels and drove machines linked to water wheels.

Steam power was quite a new discovery in 1826 when six steamboats were trading between Limerick and Athlone. But steam power was not yet used in industry.

Years passed and Shannon was an idle river. Its waters poured uselessly into the Atlantic Ocean.

In 1860 the first electric dynamo was invented. Sixty-two years later important events took place in Ireland. In 1922 the country was declared a Free State within the British Commonwealth, with its own government in Dublin. The age-old dream of Ireland governed by Irishmen had at last come true. The year that brought the opportunity also produced the man to seize the opportunity. A young engineer, Thomas McLaughlin, had studied the production of electricity by waterpower in Scandinavia and Germany. He dreamed and he schemed and he gained the ear of the new government, men of vision and enthusiasm who loved their country.

A scheme to harness the waters of the Shannon for electric power was approved, and money was made available for the work. McLaughlin and his fellow engineers approached a German firm which prepared a plan. The work was started and equipment, engineers, technicians, contractors and laborers arrived on the site.

The plan was to build a dam below Killaloe and divert the river into a canal running eight miles to the power station. There the water would make the great turbines spin. From the power station

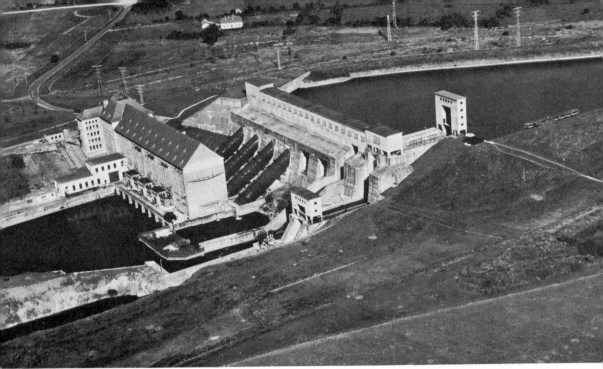

Electricity Supply Board

This is Ardnacrusha, the Shannon's first electric power plant.

a tailrace one and one-half miles long would take the water back to the riverbed above Limerick. Little by little the great dam and power station were built. They were the first ever seen in the country.

Four turbines arrived in Limerick. A difficulty arose. The winding country roads could not carry the bulky loads. So the contractors built a railroad from Limerick to carry the machinery. The tracks ran straight into the power station and are still used.

Ardnacrusha is a quiet green place. The silence is broken by the lowing of cattle or the song of a bird. The water in the headrace is still and silent. The only other sound is the hissing of the high-tension cables which stretch across the fields on steel pylons. Like giants, the pylons stride over hills and bogs, beneath the tumbling smoky clouds.

Inside the power station things are spick-and-span. The drone of the turbines fills the building. Everything vibrates, even the glass in the windows. The engineers are so used to the vibration that they notice only when it stops.

The output of the turbines is 124,000 horse-power, about four times more than the estimate of 1844. The electric age has come to Ireland.

The Shannon has always been a fine salmon, trout and eel river. Salmon feed and grow to maturity in the sea and return to the river of their birth to spawn. Eels live and feed in the river but migrate to the Sargasso Sea to spawn.

Eels are long, sinuous and slimy like snakes. Although they sometimes travel over land, they

Supervisor John Lynch sorts young fish by size at Parteen Hatchery.

are fish, not reptiles. They reach maturity at about eight years of age when they go downstream to the sea, traveling by night. They swim on to the Sargasso Sea where they mate, spawn and die. When the little eels, or elvers, hatch, they instinctively start on the long journey back to their parents' feeding grounds. Like splinters of flexible glass, they enter the river in millions.

When the big dam was finished, the fish could not come upriver to their spawning and feeding grounds. Something had to be done. The engineers built a scientific and up-to-date fish-pass on the old river, but still the fish collected in the pool at the foot of the dam.

Eventually the problem was solved. A new fish-

The hatchery can handle up to 5,000,000 salmon eggs each year.

pass, a sort of water elevator, was built. A tower not unlike an ancient round tower rises from the foot to the top of the dam. At the bottom there are openings. The fish swim into these. Every four hours a gate closes. The level of the water rises in the tower, carrying the fish to the top. They are released into the river above the dam.

Inside a passage leading from the tower to the river, electronic machines count the number and record the size of salmon returning to spawn.

Above the power station at Parteen Weir, the Fisheries Section of the Electricity Supply Board has a salmon hatchery. The fish are stripped of their spawn and returned to the river. The fertilized spawn is hatched in tanks, and the baby fish are fed on minced liver until they are a year old and three or four inches long. Then they are released into the river. Mortality among tiny salmon hatched in the river is high—about 80%. The hatchery protects the small fish until they have a good chance of survival.

The Fisheries Section has the right to 28% of all fish ascending the river. Fresh-run salmon are killed by electrocution in Limerick. Killed this way, they are in top condition for eating, fresh from the sea, unmarked and not exhausted from the journey upstream.

The remaining 72% continue their journey and are netted or caught by sportsmen with rod and line.

Salmon should be cooked and eaten very soon after being taken from the river. River people say, "It should be cooked with the tide in it"— that is, before the turn of the tide. In many a house it is the rule that any fish brought home is cooked before the fisherman or his wife may go to bed. Anyone who has eaten fresh-caught salmon wouldn't give a second look at the flabby pink fish sold in the shops.

Salmon fishing on the Shannon has been important for centuries. Records show that when Limerick was besieged by the English in the seventeenth century a truce was arranged during a heavy run of fish so the fishermen could fish in safety. It is pretty certain that the Irish soldiers laid aside their arms and joined in the sport.

Independent Newspapers Ltd.

Limerick, where the Irish fought and won with pitchforks and bottles.

9. Gateway to the Sea

From Ardnacrusha the Shannon tumbles along
into Limerick, one of the oldest and proudest
cities in Ireland. John, Lord of Ireland and later
King of England, granted it a charter in 1197,

and it had a mayor even before London did. Long before King John's time, it was a Danish town. Even now there is a weir on the river known as the Laks Weir. Lak is still the Danish word for a salmon.

The records of the city are full of interesting bits of information. In 1290 tallow candles were first used. In 1379 wool cloth was first made there, and 38 years later paper was first made out of rags.

In 1495 it was decreed that any subject having goods to the value of £20 must have "A Jack, Sallet and English bow and sheaf of arrows, and every freeholder a horse also to assist the King." A jack and sallet were the protective garment and helmet worn by archers.

Uniforms for the Confederate Army in the United States were made in Limerick by a firm still in existence.

In the seventeenth century Limerick, which was a walled city, was besieged by English troops. When the walls were breached by cannon fire, men, women and children attacked the English with homemade weapons: hatchets, pitchforks, sticks, stones, pickaxes, broken bottles and even brooms. They fought in every street, alley and passageway with such terrible ferocity that the enemy retreated in absolute confusion. The soldiers could not be made to return to the attack. They struck camp and left the battered but triumphant city in peace.

History tells of a balloon ascent made over Limerick in 1789. Probably the very first description of the Shannon River from the air is that of another balloonist in 1849. He brought a barometer with him, and it recorded that the balloon rose to a height of 4,261 feet. He complained of finding it hard to breathe at this height. He didn't have any parachute so perhaps he was just too scared to breathe.

He wrote, "The expanse of view of the various windings of the Shannon was little interrupted, being visible to Killaloe. Large fields looked like pocket handkerchieves." He noted also, "A sad waste of land there was under stone walls marking subdivision of property."

Tillable land in Ireland is still wasted under countless stone walls.

The mention of subdivided fields is of special interest. In that year, 1849, the Shannon country and the whole of Ireland were emerging from one of the most terrible disasters of history—The Great Famine. It affected the history of Ireland and also of Canada and the United States.

Ireland had always been a farming country, with more people living on farms than in the towns. The farms had been divided and subdivided by the great landlords, many of whom lived in England. They had little interest in their Irish lands except to draw rents from them. The rents were collected ruthlessly by their agents. Failure to pay meant that the farmer would be put out of his home. The peasant farmer had to sell every beast he raised and every crop he grew to keep his roof over his head. He could keep only the potatoes, which were the chief food eaten by his family.

Potatoes were planted in March and could be eaten in July. The only tool a farmer needed was a spade. The potato crop was stored for winter use and also fed to animals.

In 1845 the potato crop failed. Potato blight turned the plants to black rotten pulp. For three more years the same thing happened.

Famine came, and with it disease. Boatloads of corn, cattle, pigs and dairy produce still went down the Shannon for export to England. The people had no money to buy food or clothes and from the riverbanks they watched hopelessly. They were fever-ridden, filthy, half-naked and crazed with hunger. In rotten, crowded boats they traveled the river to the towns where the famine relief centers gave them a little food. It was scarcely enough to keep the life in them. Sometimes the boats sank. In one case 39 bodies were washed ashore, and the report in the papers said piously, "Heaven awarded them a more merciful death than starvation."

The townspeople and the richer farmers helped all they could, but there were too many hungry mouths for them to feed. The peasants ate weeds, berries, dug for roots and even ate grass. They died, and there were few strong enough to bury them. There was a stench of rotting potatoes and death over the slow-moving river.

Some managed to borrow money for the fare to America. Some of the landlords, anxious to rid themselves of penniless tenants, exported them to Canada and the U.S.A. It was cheaper and less trouble than feeding them.

Many of the boats were unseaworthy. Others were ships used for importing timber from Canada. The emigrants made fine ballast in the outgoing boats. Human ballast cost nothing to unload. From Limerick many of these sad ships sailed. Coffin ships they were called, because so many died on them. A million people died and three million others left the country in those four years.

Those who survived the nightmare voyages were not welcome in Canada and the U.S.A. The authorities were not unkind, but it was difficult to know what to do with thousands of starving, dirty people, especially since many of them had the dreaded typhus fever.

The young and the strong took any work they could get. They built railroads, worked in mines, made roads, fought with the army and sailed with the navy. They were the "poor whites," the volunteer slave labor of the New World.

The Irish emigrants brought nothing with them but their faith, their laughter and their fierce pride of race. Their descendants gradually gained a place in American society, and a strong bond of affection grew between the people of the great continent and those of the little green island in the Atlantic.

The Irish poet, Emily Lawless, wrote of Ireland's emigrants:

(Ireland speaks:)
She said, I never called them sons,
I almost ceased to breathe their name,
Then caught it echoing down the wind,
Blown backwards from the winds of Fame.

Happily those times are long past. Limerick on the Shannon is a gay modern city. Automobiles line the streets, neon lights flash, well-dressed cheerful people of many nationalities go on their way.

On the river, ships come and go. Yachts, cruisers and dinghies rise and fall with the ebb and flow of the tide. Young men in slender racing craft scull up and down the river. Gulls scream and wheel above the town and swans glide on the river.

How a 19th century American artist portrayed the potato crop failure.

Anglers fish from the bridges as the traffic hurries by. King John's Castle stands guard over Thomond Bridge where the silvery fish leap and splash. It is here that the Electricity Supply Board takes its share of salmon. Sinister black cormorants dive for fish. They get a poor welcome because they eat more than their fair share and prefer tender young salmon.

Limerick is a city of bells. At dawn, at noon and at evening time the bells of its many churches peal out over the city.

A double-deck bus and Georgian houses on O'Connell Street, Limerick.

Limerick is famous for its bacon, its butter and cream. Truckloads of milk cans and squealing pigs rattle through the streets.

It is fun to ride upstairs on a double-deck bus. Like a rajah on his elephant or a sheik on his camel, one can look down on everybody else.

Things which the driver of an expensive motorcar cannot see are on view to the buyer of a four-penny bus ticket.

There is a view of the other man's back garden, his hen run, the washing on the line, the baby in the pram. There is even a glimpse through the elegant windows of the tall, dusky-brick Georgian houses which have beautiful fanlights over the doors.

Crossing Thomond Bridge on the top deck of a bus gives a bird's-eye view of the boats, the open hatches, the coiled ropes, and the sailors working or lounging. Laden ships of 10,000 tons berth at the quays. Timber, grain and coal are the import cargoes handled. Bacon and condensed milk are exported. A pneumatic elevator unloads the grain speedily. The giant cranes swing and rattle over the docks, and the voices of foreign seamen mix with the Limerick voices as they have for hundreds of years.

Irish Tourist Board

Bunratty Castle

10.
West to the Atlantic

Eight miles west of Limerick the river broadens out into the estuary which is one-and-a-half miles wide, and deep enough for ships of 10,000 tons.

A hundred yards from the river on the north bank stands Bunratty Castle. All who wished to travel upriver, whether friend or foe, had first to pass this point which was fortified by the Celts, Danes, English and the Irish themselves.

The castle which towers over the river is the fourth of its name and is more than 400 years old. It has immensely thick walls and three main halls one above the other. At each corner is a tower with six rooms. At the top of a flight of steps is a drawbridge and the main entrance.

The door is only wide enough to admit one person at a time. Over the door is a slit in the ceiling called a "murder hole." Callers were carefully inspected through this hole. If they were unwelcome, they were stabbed or doused with boiling water. Inside is the hall called the Main Guard where the soldiers lived. A famous military man in command of the castle 300 years ago was Admiral Sir William Penn. He was the father of William Penn, Quaker founder of Pennsylvania. As a boy Penn lived at Bunratty with his father.

The private rooms and chapels were in the towers, which are as high as an eight-story building. Near one roof was a pigeon loft. Fresh meat was often scarce in winter, and the castle folk ate many of the birds.

The spiral staircases in three of the towers have a left-hand twist. A defender on the stair would therefore have a free sweep of his sword arm while the attacker below would be cramped. Going visiting uninvited was a risky business in those days.

For many years Bunratty was neglected and

This chandelier at Bunratty Castle is a mermaid held aloft by a cable.

Shannon Free Airport

Nine lovely ladies sing for the suppers in Bunratty's Main Guard.

forlorn, but today flags fly from the towers, lights shine from the windows and the sound of music and laughter drifts across the green fields and silver river. The castle came to life again when Lord Gort, its owner, gave it to the Irish nation. The building was entirely restored and furnished with valuable medieval furniture such as would have been there in the time of the Great Earl of Thomond, whose home it was. Rich tapestries, old armor and portraits of former residents hang on the walls.

By day the sun shines through stained glass windows, spilling pools of glowing color on the stone floors. On summer nights guests are welcomed to medieval banquets. They are met by pretty girls dressed in gowns of the sixteenth century, who offer them the bread of friendship. "May health and safety be with you," is their greeting. Above, in the Great Hall, the visitors are received by a make-believe Earl of Thomond and his Lady. Standing by a fire in the center of the hall, they drink a toast of spiced wine.

The feast is served below in the Main Guard, lit by flickering candles. Beside the huge fireplace gather musicians who will entertain the company. At their feet lies a wolfhound, descendant of the hunting dogs of the chieftains. The girls tie big white bibs around the diners' necks. "Fingers were made before forks" is the rule at this meal, which is eaten from wooden platters.

Meat is cut with a dagger. Brose, as the soup is called, is drunk from a bowl. Tankards are kept filled with mead and claret. Mead, which is made from fermented honey, yeast and water, used to be drunk only at weddings and other special occasions. After the meal the guests are entertained with stories, songs and dances, and everyone joins in the singing.

There are white vapor streaks in the sky over quiet Bunratty and a few miles away is the roar and bustle of Shannon Airport, one of the world's busiest airfields. The airport is only one flying hour from London and five and one-half from New York. It is rarely closed by the fogs which affect many European airports.

Opposite Kilrush on the north bank of the estuary is Scattery Island. Scat is the Danish word for a treasure, and it was the Danes who named the island Treasure Island. It was also the Danes who stole gold, silver and precious manuscripts from St. Senan's monastery. The ruins of seven churches and a round tower can still be seen on the island. Cattle and rabbits thrive on its 170 acres of rich grassland. Rabbits are rare on the mainland since the killer disease, myxomatosis, came to Ireland. Scattery rabbits were saved by being a watery mile from the mainland.

The men of the island were always great sailors. Many knew the river so well that they worked as pilots on the big ships going in and out of Limerick. Now only one family lives there. No children laugh and call. Ivy smothers the walls. Jackdaws, owls and bats flit through the arched windows of the ruined churches. The local postman travels to the mainland to collect his own mail. There is no one else left.

Scattery Island has ruins (round tower, center) but just one family.
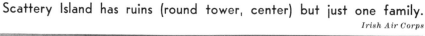
Irish Air Corps

The mainland coast at the mouth of the estuary, which is nine miles wide, has been carved into weird shapes by furious Atlantic gales. The name of one town, Ballybunion, means the "Hole of the Nine Daughters." The legend has it that these nine daughters of a local chieftain used to sneak down to the beach to meet handsome Vikings. When their father found out, he was so angry that he threw the nine of them into a blowhole under the cliffs. Today children play on the golden sands and seals sun themselves on the rocks. Each year seals eat thousands of salmon coming up the Shannon to spawn.

The black rocks of Ballybunion, near the mouth of the River Shannon.

Irish Tourist Board

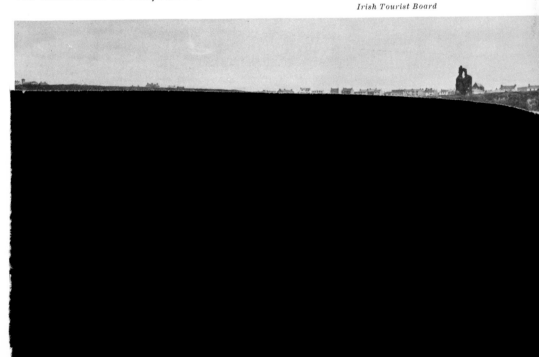

Stories are told of a sunken island in the mouth of the river, an island with golden palaces and shining towers, an island with green fields and fragrant flowers. Indeed some fishermen used to tell that as they rowed their boats they could smell the flowers of the fields below. Every seven years the island is supposed to rise above the waves for a short time but those who see it will not be alive to see it seven years later.

Fourteen hundred years ago St. Brendan, the navigator, sailed westward to seek the Isles of the Blest and saw many strange things. It is believed that he reached the New World before the Vikings, who went there from Iceland.

St. Brendan is still honored by those traveling west. An Irish airliner bearing his name soars into the air, circles the airport and speeds westward. Eager young eyes look down hopefully yet

The name of St. Brendan the navigator is borne by this Aer Lingus jet.

Index

Allen, Lough, 9, 14, 19, 20
Ardnacrusha, 10, 14, 67, 69, 70, 75
Arigna Generating Station, 20
Arigna Mountain, 16
Athlone, 11, 40–45, 67
Athlone Castle, 45
Atlantic Ocean, 8, 11

Balloon ascension, 77
Ballybunion, 93
Bards, 61, 62
Boating, 11, 12, 42, 55, 59, 63, 82
Boderg, Lough, 24
Bogs, 30, 31, 34, 36, 37
Bog butter, 32, 33
Books, 47, 48
Bov Dearg, 27, 29
Brendan, St., 94, 95
Brigid, St., 57, 59
Bronze, 14, 16
Brose, 91
Bunratty Castle, opposite title
    page, 86–91
    Main Guard, 87, 89, 90
Buses, 84, 85

Callows, 56
Canada, 78, 80, 81
Catholics, 40
Celts, 17, 86
Churches, 45, 55, 83, 91
Ciaran, St., 45, 48, 51
Clonmacnoise, 45–47, 51
Coal, 16, 36
Cob, 23
Coffin ships, 81

Connacht, 40, 41, 43, 44
Copper, 16
Cot, 56
County Cavan, 7, 13
Crannog, 15
Cromwell, Oliver, 40, 41
Custume, Sergeant, 44
Cygnets, 23, 24

Danes, 48, 50, 54, 55, 62, 86, 91
Dapping, 63–65
Demons, 19
Denmark, 12
Derg, Lough, 9, 61, 63, 64, 67
Dergderc, Lough, 62
Donkeys, 35, 38, 39
Dublin, 60, 63, 68
Dun, 17

Eels, 70–72
Electricity, 30, 37, 67
Electricity Supply Board, 73, 83
England, 19, 38, 79
Eva, 27–29

Famine, 78–83
Farming, 13, 15, 38, 56, 66, 79
Fionnuala, 26–28
Fishing, 20, 22, 63–65, 74, 83
Fish-pass, 72, 73
Fly boats, 60

Gaels, 6
Gold, 16
Grand Canal, 60

Hart's-Tongue fern, 10

Henry II, 40
Henry VIII, 40
Horses, 38
Hydroelectric plant, 10

Ice Age, 15
Iceland, 94
Ireland
    Description, 6, 8, 11, 30
    History, 14–19, 38, 40, 41,
        48–50, 54, 55, 61–63, 68,
        75, 78–82, 89
Iron, 17

Killaloe, 63, 64, 67, 68, 77
King John, 76
King John's Castle, 83

Lake of the Bloody Eye, 62, 66
Lanesborough, 37, 51
Lawless, Emily, 82
Legends, 6, 17, 19, 26–29, 51,
    62, 93, 94
Leslie, Lionel, 53
Limerick, opposite title page, 10,
    11, 40, 67, 69, 74–77, 81–85, 92
Lir, 26, 29
Little People, 6, 17
London, 63, 76, 91

McLaughlin, Thomas, 68
Malachy, 54, 55
Manufacturing, 36–39, 41, 76
Mayfly, 63–65
Mead, 90
Monster, 51–54

National Museum of Dublin, 12, 15
New York, 91
Normandy, 40
Normans, 40, 50
Norway, 12

Ornaments, 15
Owenmore River, 13

Parteen Hatchery, 71
Patrick, St., 19, 21
Peat, 30–38
Pen, 23
Penn, William, 87
Pollution, 11
Potato crop failure, 78–83

Poteen, 8
Protestants, 40

Queen Elizabeth, 40

Rabbits, 91, 92
Rath, 17
Ree, Lough, 9, 37, 40, 51–56, 59
    Monster of, 51–54
Round towers, 45, 48–50, 91
Rushes, 57–59

Salmon, 20, 70, 73, 74, 83
Scattery Island, 91, 92
Seals, 93
Shannon
    Description, 5, 7, 11, 13, 14,
        30–33, 38, 40, 59, 70, 82
    Geography, 7–10, 14, 30, 40,
        51, 60, 67, 75, 86
    History, 12, 40, 42, 54, 94
    Map, 4
    Name, 5
    Travel route, 11, 12, 45
    Use for electric power, 67–70,
        72–74
Shannon Dam, 69, 72
Shannon Harbour, 60
Shannon Pot, 5, 7–9, 13
Sineann, 6, 7
Slane, 32, 34
Snakes, 19
Sod, 34–36
Sphagnum, 31
Steam power, 67
Stone walls, 77
Swans, 23–28

Thomond Bridge, 83, 85
Turbary rights, 33
Turf, 31–38, 60
Turf Board, 33, 35, 36, 38
Turgesius the Dane, 54, 55
Turloughs, 57

United States of America, 76,
    78, 80, 81

Vikings, 12, 48, 49, 54, 93

William III, 42
Wolfhounds, 18, 19

Meet the Author

NORA NOWLAN was raised on a farm at the foot of one of the Dublin Mountains. As a child, she explored the countryside on horseback, on foot and by bicycle, and fished for brown trout and pinkeens in the nearby streams. She attended schools in Ireland and Scotland, and later married K. I. Nowlan, a Dublin lawyer and town planner. The Nowlans and their five children live on a farm, where they breed Jersey cattle, raise poultry and tomatoes for market, and enjoy their view of the Dublin Mountains.

The Shannon is Mrs. Nowlan's first children's book. She writes: "American friends visiting us suggested that I write a book. . . . 'I couldn't,' I said. 'Well, try,' they insisted. They won. I went to an auction and bought an ancient typewriter for ten dollars and learned to type with two fingers. Later, we hired a caravan, and my husband, our two youngest sons and I set off in search of the Shannon Pot. On the journey I rediscovered all the magic of the mountains, rivers and countryside of Ireland."